Most Outrageous Hoaxes

Judy Coghill

Series Editor
Jeffrey D. Wilhelm

Much thought, debate, and research went into choosing and ranking the 10 items in each book in this series. We realize that everyone has his or her own opinion of what is most significant, revolutionary, amazing, deadly, and so on. As you read, you may agree with our choices, or you may be surprised — and that's the way it should be!

an imprint of

SCHOLASTIC

www.scholastic.com/librarypublishing

A Rubicon book published in association with Scholastic Inc.

Rubicon © 2007 Rubicon Publishing Inc.
www.rubiconpublishing.com

Associate Publishers: Kim Koh, Miriam Bardswich
Project Editor: Amy Land
Editor: Dona Foucault
Creative Director: Jennifer Drew
Project Manager/Designer: Jeanette MacLean
Graphic Designer: Jen Harvey

The publisher gratefully acknowledges the following for permission to reprint copyrighted material in this book.

Every reasonable effort has been made to trace the owners of copyrighted material and to make due acknowledgment. Any errors or omissions drawn to our attention will be gladly rectified in future editions.

"Letter From Sir Arthur Conan Doyle to Mr. Wright," courtesy of James Randi Educational Foundation.

"Bonsai Kittens, Anyone?" by Larry O'Hanlon, *Discovery News*, November 3, 2003. Used with permission.

Cover image: Alien–Getty Images/The Image Bank/Antonio M Rosario; PhotoDisc

Library and Archives Canada Cataloguing in Publication

Coghill, Judy, 1948-
        The 10 most outrageous hoaxes/Judy Coghill.

 Includes index.
ISBN 978-1-55448-476-8

        1. Readers (Elementary) 2. Readers—Impostors and imposture.
I. Title. II. Title: Ten most outrageous hoaxes.

PE1117.C625 2007   428.6   C2007-900544-6

1 2 3 4 5 6 7 8 9 10   10   16 15 14 13 12 11 10 09 08 07

Printed in Singapore

Contents

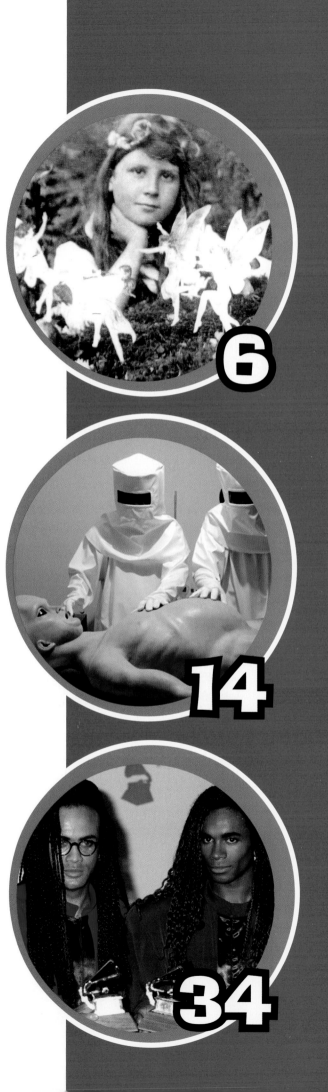

YOU'VE BEEN

Has someone ever played a prank on you? What made you fall for it? How did you feel once you found out you'd been tricked?

Playing pranks is such a part of human nature that there's even a day devoted to its celebration: April Fool's Day (the first day of April). Of course, a true prankster would never waste the other 364 days!

Like pranks, hoaxes are created for many reasons. Sometimes a hoax takes the shape of a joke and is harmless and even fun. At other times, the hoax gets out of control and people get in trouble or die. In this book, we've gathered 10 of the most outrageous hoaxes of all time and ranked them according to originality, media attention, entertainment value, method of distribution, their place in time, the time and thought put into making them happen, and the number of people fooled. As well, we considered the enduring nature of the hoax and its impact on those who had been punk'd.

As you read the selections in this book, think of all the pranks and tricks you know. What made them work and why?

PUNK'D!

WHAT DO YOU THINK IS THE MOST OUTRAGEOUS HOAX?

10 COTTINGLEY

Frances with the fairies — photograph taken by her cousin, Elsie, in July 1917

FAIRIES

THE GRANGER COLLECTION, NEW YORK

WHERE: Cottingley, Yorkshire, England

WHEN: 1917

BELIEVE IT OR NOT: Two young girls claimed they saw fairies in their backyard. Even Sir Arthur Conan Doyle, the famous writer of the Sherlock Holmes detective stories, believed their story!

Elsie Wright, 16 years old, and Frances Griffiths, her 10-year-old cousin, had fairies as friends. And they had photographs to prove it — taken with a camera that belonged to Elsie's father.

These photographs showed the girls playing with fairies. There were various poses showing Elsie and Frances in different activities with small, winged female creatures hovering above and around them.

Once the pictures were made public, many people believed the fairies were cutouts suspended on wires. The girls denied that, and people believed them. After all, how could such lovely, young, innocent-looking girls be lying? What did they know about faking photographs? Photography was a new art form then. Not many people understood its technology well enough to know that photos could be faked.

The girls became famous, especially when *Sherlock Holmes*'s author, Sir Arthur Conan Doyle, believed the photos were real. He even wrote about them in his book *The Coming of the Fairies*.

? Sir Arthur Conan Doyle's belief in the fairies made the hoax even more credible. Why do you think this is?

COTTINGLEY FAIRIES

WHY IT HAPPENED

It was a prank that got out of hand. This was a time soon after World War I, when people had experienced hardship, suffering, devastation, and death. Fairies reminded them of folklore and magical powers. News of these beautiful creatures provided a welcome relief after the war.

devastation: *widespread destruction*

Photograph of Elsie Wright

ALL PROFITS ON SALE GIVEN TO THE QUEEN'S "WORK FOR WOMEN" FUND

PRINCESS MARY'S GIFT BOOK

BUCKINGHAM PALACE

I desire to express my very best thanks to the Authors and Artists who have so generously contributed to my Gift Book.

Mary

Price Two Shillings and Sixpence net

HODDER & STOUGHTON, PUBLISHERS, ST. PAUL'S HOUSE, WARWICK SQUARE, LONDON, E.C.

THE CLUES

From the beginning, many photography experts had their doubts. In 1978, a researcher noticed that the fairies in the pictures were almost identical to fairy illustrations in a 1915 book called *Princess Mary's Gift Book*.

BUSTED!

In 1981, the two cousins, by then senior citizens, confessed to writer Joe Cooper that the fairy pictures were indeed cutouts from the 1915 children's book. They had pinned the cutouts to the ground and to branches. They admitted the photographs were fakes.

The Expert Says...

"We must either believe in the almost incredible mystery of the fairy or in the almost incredible wonders of the faked photographs."

— *City News*, January 29, 1921

10   9   8   7   6

June 30, 1919

To: Arthur Wright

This 1919 letter from Sir Arthur Conan Doyle to Elsie's father shows how excited the Sherlock Holmes writer was about proving that fairies exist.

Quick Fact

Paramount Pictures made a movie about this hoax entitled *Fairy Tale: A True Story*, released in 1997.

Dear Mr. Wright,

I have seen the very interesting photos which your little girl took. They are certainly amazing. I was writing a little article for the *Strand* upon the evidence for the existence of fairies, so that I was very much interested. I should naturally like to use the photos, along with other material, in my article but would not of course do so without your knowledge and permission. It would be in the Xmas number.

I suggest

1. That no name be mentioned, so that neither you nor your daughter be annoyed in any way.
2. That the use be reserved for the *Strand* only until Xmas. After that it reverts of course to you.
3. That either £5 be paid to you by the *Strand* for the temporary use, or that if you don't care to take money, you be put on the free list of the magazine for five years.

The articles appear in America in connection with the *Strand* publication. I would, if you agree, try to get you another £5 from that side. If this is all agreeable to you I or my friend Mr. Gardner would try to run up & have half an hour's chat with the girls.

Yours sincerely

A. Conan Doyle

reverts: *goes back*

Take Note

The Cottingley Fairies hoax ranks #10 on our list. It was not elaborate or brilliant, but it created interest and controversy for over 60 years. The girls simply used paper cutouts of fairies in their photos, but the images remain one of the most famous photographic hoaxes of all time.

• Do you think someone would be able to pull a photography hoax like this today in view of modern photographic equipment and computer technology? Explain.

One spectator said he knew there was a problem as soon as he saw Ruiz cross the finish line—she didn't even look tired!

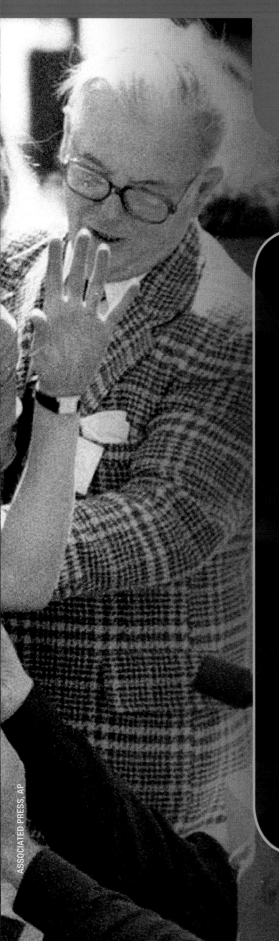

WHERE: Boston, Massachusetts

WHEN: April 21, 1980

BELIEVE IT OR NOT: Rosie Ruiz was named the winner of the 1980 Boston Marathon, even though she only ran a few miles!

Rosie Ruiz was declared the female winner of the 1980 Boston Marathon, the world's most famous long-distance race. She won the race with a record time of 2 hours, 31 minutes, and 56 seconds.

Who was Ruiz? Questions started flying immediately after her victory. Jacqueline Gareau, a Canadian, was the recognized leader in the women's division. Imagine Gareau's amazement when she arrived at the finish line just in time to see Ruiz crowned the champion!

Some spectators came forward, saying they saw Ruiz leap from the crowd and join the race in the last stretch to sprint to the finish. Others said Ruiz appeared fresh and had barely broken a sweat. "I know a top runner when I see one. She didn't look tired," said one runner. "Her face was not even flushed," said another.

"I ran the race. I really did," said a tearful Ruiz. She offered to submit to a lie-detector test.

The race was captured on film, and there were thousands of photographs of the marathon. Eight days and 10,000 photographs later, race officials declared that Rosie Ruiz had not run the race. It was a hoax!

 What made this one of the most famous hoaxes of the 20th century?

ROSIE RUIZ

WHY IT HAPPENED

Rosie Ruiz has always denied cheating in the race. Doug Darling, in a 2006 article in the *Orlando Sentinel*, wrote that many think she never intended to win the race. Rather, she just wanted to run well enough to impress her New York employers. She had told them she was an expert runner.

THE CLUES

She wasn't sweating, no one could remember running next to her, and she wasn't in any of the photos or video footage of the race.

Quick Fact

As the story goes, Rosie Ruiz rode the subway to join the race within less than a mile from the finish line. No one can do that now. All runners have computerized chips on their shoes to track the time they start and end a race.

Rosie Ruiz crosses the finish line in the women's division of the Boston Marathon, April 21, 1980.

? Are there any circumstances under which cheating is justified? Explain your answer.

BUSTED!

It was one of the most famous hoaxes of the 20th century. Rosie Ruiz was disqualified and stripped of her title. Second-place finisher Jacqueline Gareau was declared the rightful winner. Further investigations led to the discovery that Ruiz had also cheated in her qualifying race, the New York Marathon. She was banned from all major marathons.

The Expert Says...

" ... the history she really made was as a cheater with unparalleled swagger. "

— Dean Juipe, sports columnist, *Las Vegas Sun*, January 28, 2000

? How does Ruiz's "unparalleled swagger," or unapologetic attitude to being caught cheating, make this hoax more outrageous?

MARATHON NOTEBOOK

Rosie Ruiz's Boston Marathon hoax generated a lot of controversy and talk. Check out these quotations about the race for more insight.

"Jacqueline Gareau is happy with her life. At 47, she devotes most of her time to her 7 1/2-year-old son, Yannick; has taken up cycling, and is enjoying the journey of growing older and 'learning to sit still.'"

— Barbara Huebner,
Globe Correspondent, April 16, 2000

Canada's Jacqueline Gareau crosses a ceremonial finish line in Boston, 25 years after her victory.

"I knew for sure that I was the winner. I just thought I was first until I heard someone tell me I was second. ... I couldn't understand how she could pass me."

— Jacqueline Gareau, 1980

"I wish she [Ruiz] has more wisdom. ... Boston will always be something for me. ... It's like I've made more friends that way than if I would have won right away."

— Gareau celebrating the 20th anniversary of her 1980 win that almost wasn't

"I saw a woman stumble out of the crowd. ... She was wearing a number. I didn't take her very seriously. I watched her stumble along the right-hand side of the street."

— John Faulkner,
a witness to the hoax, 1980

Take Note

The Boston Marathon hoax in 1980 takes the #9 position because it wasn't particularly well planned. The runners and spectators had suspicions immediately after Rosie Ruiz was declared the winner. However, the hoax had a significant impact on Jacqueline Gareau, who lost out on her winning moment. It also affected the winner of the men's race, whose victory was overshadowed by the scandal.

• Aside from being disqualified from running in future marathons, Rosie Ruiz wasn't ever charged with a crime. Do you think she should have been? Why or why not?

5   4   3   2   1

Scene from Alien Autopsy, a 2006 movie that is a humorous remake of the Santilli film

SY

WHERE: American television studio

WHEN: August 28, 1995

BELIEVE IT OR NOT: This film of an alien autopsy played on the belief among some people that there are life-forms on other planets.

In 1947, many people saw what they believed was a UFO crash landing in Roswell, New Mexico. They also believed the military and the government were trying to keep the landing a secret. Some even suspected that an alien had been taken from the UFO and was secretly being held captive.

The military claimed the debris found at Roswell was the remains of a top-secret surveillance balloon that had crashed. Eyewitness descriptions of the debris found on the Roswell ranch matched descriptions of the materials from the crashed military balloon. However, many people continued to believe that a flying saucer did crash in Roswell.

Then, almost 40 years later, Ray Santilli, a film producer and director, revealed a tape that he had purchased from an ex-army photographer. It showed the autopsy of an alien at Fort Worth Army Air Field. The photographer claimed the alien was captured from the flying saucer that crashed in Roswell in 1947.

An American television network aired the film on August 28, 1995. So, was the film real or was it a hoax?

ALIEN AUTOPSY

WHY IT HAPPENED

Santilli insisted that the original film was real. He admitted that he did have to re-create most of it after the original film was damaged in storage. Others believed he might just have wanted the fame and the money that went along with it.

Quick Fact

John Humphreys, a sculptor and special-effects expert from Manchester, England, now claims that the Roswell alien was his handiwork. Humphreys has done work on films like *Alexander* and *Charlie and the Chocolate Factory*.

Alien autopsy exhibit in the Roswell Museum

Quick Fact

The television network that aired the Santilli film later produced a program claiming the alien autopsy was a hoax.

THE CLUES

Surgeons, scientists, and filmmakers saw many inconsistencies in the film. The alien looked like a special-effects dummy; surgical procedures and instruments were incorrectly used; close-ups of the internal organs were out of focus — maybe on purpose?

BUSTED!

On April 4, 2006, in a British documentary called *Eamonn Investigates: Alien Autopsy*, Santilli and fellow film producer Gary Shoefield said that about five percent of the film was original. They admitted the rest was a re-creation from original footage that had deteriorated. Experts generally agree that this autopsy is a hoax.

inconsistencies: *things that don't make sense*

? If Santilli had revealed this information in 1995, would people have been more, or less, willing to believe the autopsy had happened?

The Expert Says...

"Television executives have a responsibility not to confuse programs designed for entertainment with news documentaries. They ought not ... mislead the public."

— Paul Kurtz, founder of the Committee for the Scientific Investigation of Claims of the Paranormal (CSICOP)

10 9 **8** 7 6

HOAX DETECTING 101

Still worried you might not be able to tell the truth from a hoax? This flowchart will help you bust the hoax before it makes a fool of you.

Credibility through association: The storyteller begins by saying this happened to a friend or a friend of a friend. This creates credibility through association. Also, the storyteller generally uses quite a serious and dramatic tone.

credibility: ability to be believed

Technical language: Many hoaxes, especially e-mail hoaxes, are told or written as if they came from someone with authority. A lot of technical jargon tends to make people believe the story is real. A bit of online research can usually help you pick out the errors or lies.

jargon: technical words that are most often used by experts

Based in reality: The story will usually start with something quite believable, and often not all that exciting. For example, you get a phone message that tells you to press certain numbers on the phone keypad to win a prize. Or, a friend of a friend went to the grocery store to buy some lettuce.

Obvious clues: Any story that starts with "this is really true" or an e-mail that starts with "send this to all your friends" is probably a hoax.

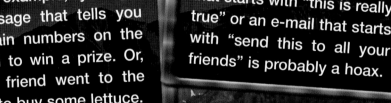

Unbelievable: The story eventually becomes extraordinary. For example, when those keypad numbers are touched, someone can now charge all of his or her long distance calls to your number. Or, the lettuce purchased at the grocery store had a frog in it that grew from the tadpoles that were in the original water ... a little far-fetched!

Take Note

Because the creation of the dummy alien and the filming of the "autopsy" require considerable skill and cleverness, the Alien Autopsy ranks #8, higher than the Rosie Ruiz hoax. Even today, the Santilli film still has many experts arguing about whether or not there was a real alien autopsy.
• Is the entertainment value of a hoax like the alien autopsy more important than the truth? Why?

5   4   3   2   1

Tourists still regularly come to see the house at 112 Ocean Drive, much to the annoyance of the locals who refer to them as the "Amityville Horribles."

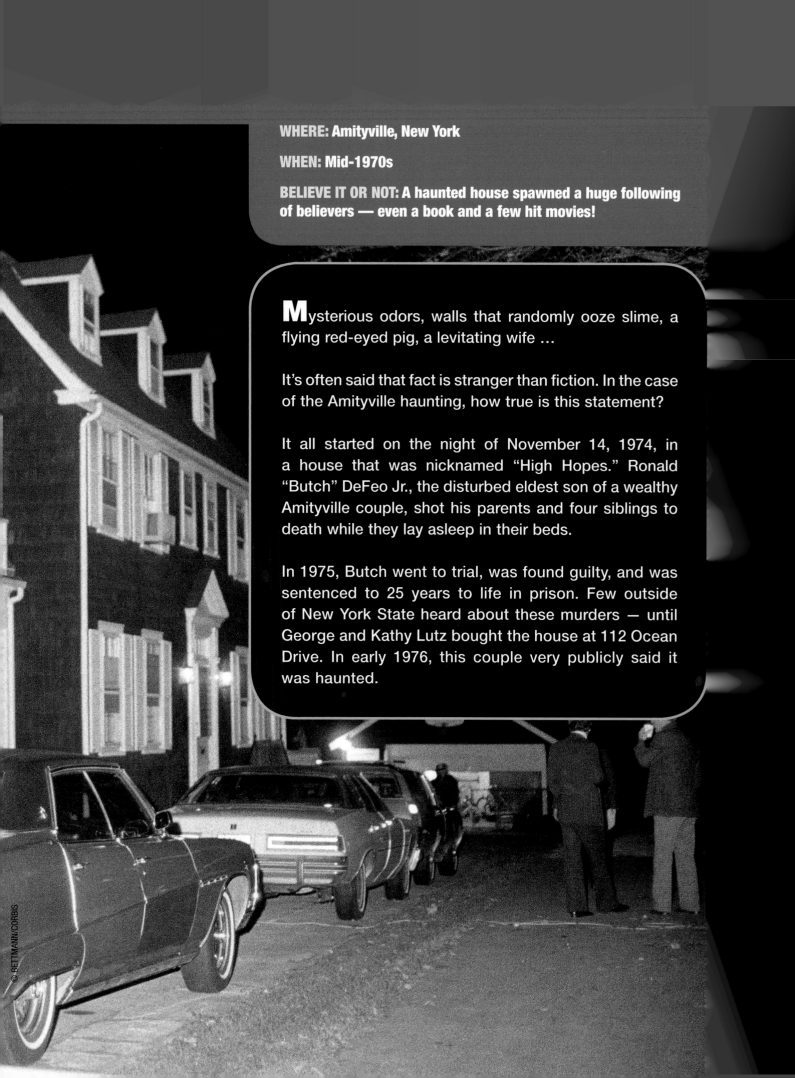

WHERE: Amityville, New York

WHEN: Mid-1970s

BELIEVE IT OR NOT: A haunted house spawned a huge following of believers — even a book and a few hit movies!

Mysterious odors, walls that randomly ooze slime, a flying red-eyed pig, a levitating wife …

It's often said that fact is stranger than fiction. In the case of the Amityville haunting, how true is this statement?

It all started on the night of November 14, 1974, in a house that was nicknamed "High Hopes." Ronald "Butch" DeFeo Jr., the disturbed eldest son of a wealthy Amityville couple, shot his parents and four siblings to death while they lay asleep in their beds.

In 1975, Butch went to trial, was found guilty, and was sentenced to 25 years to life in prison. Few outside of New York State heard about these murders — until George and Kathy Lutz bought the house at 112 Ocean Drive. In early 1976, this couple very publicly said it was haunted.

AMITYVILLE HAUNTING

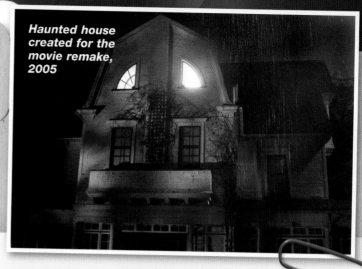

Haunted house created for the movie remake, 2005

WHY IT HAPPENED

George Lutz and his wife Kathy claimed that they were being terrorized by strange noises and that a mysterious force was ripping doors and shutters off their hinges. William Webber, Butch's lawyer, had hoped to use the haunting to try to get Butch a new trial. Webber was going to tell the judge that evil spirits made Butch murder his family. As an added bonus, Webber and the Lutzes could make some money by writing a book about the murders, the trial, and the haunting.

THE CLUES

The Lutzes, with writer Jay Anson, wrote the book called *The Amityville Horror*. It was claimed to be based on true events and became a best seller. A movie was made based on this book. Readers started to raise questions, which eventually led to the debunking of the hoax. How could there be hoofprints in the snow when there was no recorded snowfall that day? Was a priest actually terrorized by demons after visiting the house? How long did the Lutzes stay away from their house after the haunting? Did they hold a garage sale the day after they supposedly fled their house in fear of death?

debunking: *proving something to be false*

BUSTED!

The hoax was eventually uncovered. Webber admitted to his role and sued the Lutzes for $2 million for not following through on their book deal. The Lutzes eventually admitted that some of the things described in the Jay Anson book and in the movie didn't happen quite the way they were portrayed. Even Butch admitted to knowing of the hoax.

Quick Fact

Later owners of the house on Ocean Drive experienced so many problems with curiosity-seekers that they sued the Lutzes as well as author Jay Anson and the book publishers. The suit was settled out of court for an undisclosed amount of money.

? What is it about ghost stories and other unexplained phenomena that capture our interest?

The Expert Says...

" [The Amityville story is] … a blending of fact with fiction in an attempt to titillate and terrify the American public. "

— Troy Taylor, author of *Amityville: Horror or Hoax?*

titillate: *excite*

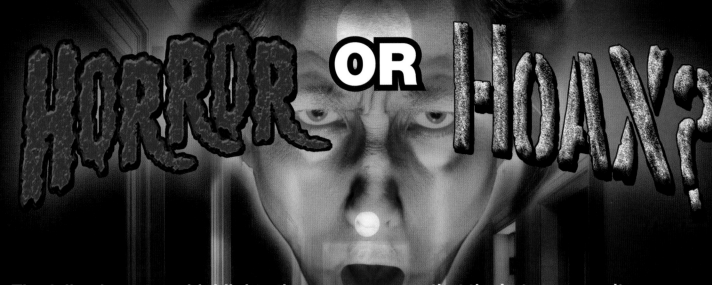

HORROR OR HOAX?

The following report highlights the many reasons that the Lutzes weren't taken seriously by an expert in the world of the supernatural.

You know you're in trouble when even the people whose business it is to believe in ghosts don't believe you! That's what happened to the Lutzes when they tried to fool Dr. Stephen Kaplan, a leading expert on the supernatural.

George Lutz called on Kaplan to investigate his haunted house on Ocean Drive. He wanted an expert to support his story that the house was indeed haunted.

George and Kathy Lutz

Kaplan was suspicious from the beginning. He said that George was vague about the supernatural activity and claimed to know nothing about the spirit world. Later in the conversation, George admitted to reading several books on demons and the supernatural world.

Kaplan told George he wouldn't charge a fee for the investigation, but if he found out the claims were false, he would tell the world. A few days later, George called Kaplan back to cancel his request.

When the Jay Anson book was published, Kaplan's doubts returned. He finally gained access to the house and found that the windows and doors were secure, not torn off their hinges, as claimed in the book. He also learned that the family returned the day after they "fled" the house and held a garage sale.

Kaplan's doubts were confirmed when William Webber, Butch's lawyer, admitted to his part in the hoax and the Lutzes confessed to making up certain parts of their story.

Take Note

Unlike the Alien Autopsy hoax, the Amityville Haunting at #7 on our list was especially cruel and insensitive. It took advantage of real murders and was a scheme developed for personal gain. The books and movies made money for the hoaxers. And people continue to believe in or be fascinated by the haunted house.

• Should people be allowed to make money from other people's misfortune? How is the Lutzes' attempt to make money from the tragedy at Ocean Drive different from Hollywood's fascination with "true-story" tragedy movies?

5   4   3   2   1

6 SWISS SPAGH

On April Fool's Day, the BBC showed a film clip of "spaghetti harvesting" in Ticino, Switzerland.

SPAGHETTI HARVEST—© BBC/CORBIS

ETTI HARVEST

WHERE: British television show

WHEN: April 1, 1957

BELIEVE IT OR NOT: A fake documentary had many viewers believing that spaghetti grows on trees. It was one of the best all-time April Fool's practical jokes.

April Fool's Day is the one day in the year when we can expect to have some pranks played on us. The joke or prank could come from anyone — friend or stranger. But would you suspect the media?

On April Fool's Day in 1957, Richard Dimbleby, the host of the British news program *Panorama*, introduced a short film clip about the unusually good spaghetti harvest in Switzerland. He credited the bountiful harvest to the demise of the tiny spaghetti weevil that had ruined crops in past years.

Viewers got to see pictures of Swiss growers picking spaghetti off the trees, putting it in their baskets, and then placing it on the slopes to dry in the sun. Dimbleby explained that due to hard work over the years, the spaghetti plant had grown well and to an even length.

The program ended with pictures of growers enjoying their harvest — plates of spaghetti! Dimbleby concluded the broadcast with, "For those who love this dish, there's nothing like real, homegrown spaghetti."

_____

weevil: *type of beetle that feeds on plants*

? What is it about human nature that makes so many people enjoy a good prank?

SWISS SPAGHETTI HARVEST

WHY IT HAPPENED

The idea for this hoax came from one of the camera operators on *Panorama*. A teacher had once told him he was so stupid he'd probably have believed that spaghetti grew on trees! Would other people believe such a thing? The British Broadcasting Corporation (BBC), the only broadcasting station at that time, decided to put it to the test. It aired the hoax on a serious TV show hosted by Richard Dimbleby, a distinguished broadcast journalist.

 Do you think a hoax such as this one would be as successful today as it was in 1957? Explain your answer.

THE CLUES

The show was aired on April Fool's Day. Viewers saw spaghetti growing on trees, and growers harvesting spaghetti. What other clues did they need?

BUSTED!

Some viewers and even a few BBC staff objected to a well-respected TV show playing such an elaborate hoax. However, most people were amused and this hoax has gone down as one of the best-ever April Fool's pranks.

? Why would people be so likely to believe a source like the BBC?

Quick Fact

The BBC received calls from a large number of viewers. They were eager to know how to grow their own spaghetti trees. The response was, "Place a sprig of spaghetti in a tin of tomato sauce and hope for the best."

Another scene from the TV program

The Expert Says...

"In an entertainment era overwhelmed by 'reality' shows, the parody and satire of the mockumentary, or 'fictional documentary,' take on even greater appeal."

— Professor Cynthia Miller, Emerson College

10   9   8   7   **6**

MEDIA MISCHIEF

Take a look at this timeline to see what famous pranks other media outlets have pulled over the years.

The Swiss spaghetti harvest hoax is believed to be the first April Fool's joke played by the media. But it wasn't the last ...

Late 1950s

Dutch television announced that the Leaning Tower of Pisa in Italy had fallen. Many shocked and upset listeners called the station for more information.

1985

George Plimpton, in a *Sports Illustrated* article, described a New York Mets recruit who could throw a fastball at 175 mph with absolute accuracy. Pretty amazing since at the time, the fastest ball ever thrown was by "power" pitcher Nolan Ryan and its speed was recorded at 100.9 mph! Even hotshot pitcher Joel Zumaya's fastest pitches are clocked at less than 105 mph.

1998

A fast-food chain advertised a burger for left-handed people. All the toppings would drip out of the right-hand side!

2005

The NASA Web site reported that water had been found on Mars. The picture on the Web site was a glass of water on a chocolate bar!

2006

A Swiss television network broadcast that the town of Fribourg was going to make drivers release their hand brakes when they parked in designated areas. This way, if parking spaces were too tight, the police could push the other cars out of the way.

Take Note

Like the Alien Autopsy at #8, this faked film footage looked real and convincing. And it was aired on a serious TV show narrated by a well-respected host. For its cleverness and originality, this one takes the #6 spot on our list.
• Go online and review the video of this hoax on the BBC Web site. Why do you think that even today, people would be impressed by this film?

5   4   3   2   1

Can you tell this photo is a hoax? Well, many people who saw it just after September 11 thought it was real!

WHERE: All over the world

WHEN: Mid-September 2001

BELIEVE IT OR NOT: Someone claimed to have found a camera in the World Trade Center rubble that contained a photo of a tourist posing on the observation deck of the World Trade Center on September 11, 2001 — as one of the hijacked jets approached from behind!

If you believe everything you read online and in your e-mail, then you probably already know the following: you'll get lead poisoning from lipstick; you'll die from inhaling free perfume samples; Nostradamus predicted 9/11; and Bill Gates wants to give you money!

The Internet has been called "the greatest medium for hoaxes of all time." Pranksters have never before had access to such a huge audience.

One of the cruelest and most unfortunate Internet-based hoaxes ever also happens to be one of the most famous: a photo that appeared to capture the final moments of a man's life on 9/11. In the photo, "Tourist Guy" posed for the camera — a regular tourist standing on top of the World Trade Center, one of the tallest buildings in the world. He had no clue what was about to happen — to him, New York City, the United States, and the world.

TOURIST GUY

WHY IT HAPPENED

This fake photo became a pop-culture sensation. The image made its way around the world when friends of the prankster forwarded it to other people after the 9/11 tragedy. People were overcome by sadness for the young man who seemed oblivious to the impending terrorist attack on the World Trade Center in New York City. So why did the young man fake the photo? He said it was purely a prank. He never meant for the photo to make its way around the world! He did not intend to deceive anyone or to seek fame this way.

 What is the most inappropriate hoax you know of? What made it inappropriate?

THE CLUES

There were many clues that the photo was a prank: the man in the photo is wearing winter clothing even though September 11, 2001, was a warm, summer day; the jet in the background is a 757, but the actual hijacked jets that hit the towers were both 767s; and the plane that hit the tower was flying in a different direction.

oblivious: *unaware*

Quick Fact

How quickly does a hoax spread? If you send an e-mail to 10 friends and then each of these friends sends it to 10 friends, the e-mail will reach one million people in six more of these cycles.

The Expert Says...

" It was supposed to be a private joke, a riff of dark humor in an anxious time. One of Guzli's friends apparently took it too far. "

— Victoria Mielke, webmaster

BUSTED!

A few weeks after the photo circulated, José Penteado, from Brazil, said he was the man in the photo. He did look like Tourist Guy, but he couldn't provide any original photos. About two months later, a Hungarian man named Peter Guzli admitted to the hoax. He took the photo of himself at the World Trade Center while on vacation. He had other photos from this trip to prove his claim. He explained that he had added the aircraft and the date onto the photograph as a joke, and sent it to his friends. It became notorious as a grim reminder of 9/11, a horrific event that struck at the heart of Americans and people around the world.

 Why would someone like José Penteado fake responsibility for such a distasteful hoax?

In August 2001, this fake photo was forwarded to thousands.

10   9   8   7   6

BONSAI KITTENS, ANYONE?

Did you know that hoaxes are such big business that many experts dedicate themselves to exposing them? Read this newspaper article for an insider's look at how the World Wide Web is playing a huge role in spreading hoaxes today.

By Larry O'Hanlon, *Discovery News*, November 3, 2003

Hoaxes are at an all time high and the Internet is largely responsible, according to a [recent] meeting of skeptics. ...

Skeptics ... gathered at the conference to debunk the latest and greatest cons, frauds, pranks, hoaxes, hauntings, UFOs, monsters, fake TV psychics, and other paranormal phenomena.

While newspapers, books, radio, and TV have all made it possible to spread hoaxes in ways early societies never dreamed possible, "they all pale in comparison to the greatest medium for hoaxes ever created — the Internet," said Alex Boese, author of the book *Museum of Hoaxes* and the Web site of the same name. ...

Another great Internet hoax that continues to suck in unsuspecting victims is "Bonsai Kitten," a Web site created by MIT students in 2000. The Web site explains how to apply Japanese "bonsai" growth control methods to kittens by stuffing felines into jars so they grow into convenient shapes. ...

Other Internet hoaxes have included fake CNN Web sites that have announced the deaths of celebrities or the auctioning on eBay of the "Ghost in a Jar." The unremarkable jar attracted hoax bids of up to $100 million before eBay pulled the plug, Boese said.

"As a species, we are very good at enchanting ourselves," explained skeptic Barry Beyerstein, a psychologist from Simon Fraser University. So it's really no surprise that despite more science and education than ever before, we keep falling for hoaxes. In fact, he said "smart people are sometimes more vulnerable because they think they are immune to being fooled."

skeptics: *people who question things many people believe are true*
vulnerable: *open to being tricked*

Take Note

What could have been seen as a cruel joke, instead, became an international sensation. Although Peter Guzli never meant for his hoax to be seen by more than a few close friends, and not much planning or expertise was required to make it happen, "Tourist Guy" comes in at #5. The reason it ranks so high on our list is that the Internet was used as the method of distribution, which means that it had the potential to fool millions of people.

• The Internet and digital technology allow almost anyone to send hoaxes out all over the world. Does this make it easier or harder to be a successful online prankster? Explain your answer.

5   4   3   2   1

4 1919 BASEBALL

A 1919 team photo of the Chicago White Sox

WORLD SERIES

WHERE: Chicago

WHEN: 1919

BELIEVE IT OR NOT: Major league baseball players lost the World Series on purpose.

The 1919 World Series was played between the Chicago White Sox and the Cincinnati Reds. The White Sox was one of the best teams that ever played. But, just before the series started, betting shifted in favor of the Reds. In the end, the White Sox lost the series 5 games to 3. Fans were shocked. How could this happen?

Chicago pitcher Chick Gandil approached small-time Chicago gambler Joseph Sullivan about fixing the 1919 World Series for $100,000. Sullivan raised the money and Gandil got the support of pitchers Eddie Cicotte and Claude "Lefty" Williams, utility infielder Fred McMullin, shortstop Charles "Swede" Risberg, and outfielders Oscar "Happy" Felsch and "Shoeless" Joe Jackson. When they received payments from Sullivan at the end of a game, they intentionally lost the next one. When no money came, they played hard and won the next game.

In 1920, the rumors surrounding the 1919 World Series wouldn't go away. So a special investigation was launched. Regretting his involvement, Cicotte decided to talk. Soon after, so did fellow team members Jackson and Williams.

Are you surprised that baseball players were involved in a scandal like this? Why?

1919 BASEBALL WORLD SERIES

WHY IT HAPPENED

The White Sox team was divided. There were two groups: one led by Eddie Collins and the other by Chick Gandil. Collins's group negotiated better salaries. This led to much bitterness. Gandil's group allegedly agreed to throw the 1919 World Series because they needed the money.

Does this type of situation justify cheating? Give reasons for your answer.

"Shoeless" Joe Jackson

THE CLUES

Chicago was the better team, but because of insider information, betting on the series suddenly shifted in the Reds' favor. Many people found it hard to believe the White Sox could have lost the series to the Reds.

BUSTED!

Eight White Sox players (and five Chicago gamblers) were charged for throwing the 1919 World Series games. The players were acquitted, though. Their signed grand jury confessions were stolen and so could not be used against them. The confessions were found years later in the possession of the club owner's lawyer.

Quick Fact

The White Sox were nicknamed Black Sox after the 1919 scandal. This nickname came from the idea that the team was "dirty."

Arnold Rothstein

Quick Fact

Although "Shoeless" Joe Jackson confessed to taking the money, he swore, right to his death, that he tried to return it and denied intentionally losing a game. He was denied entry into the Baseball Hall of Fame despite his career batting average of .356, the third highest in history.

The Expert Says...

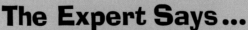

> Baseball ultimately was able to escape the Black Sox scandal relatively unscathed as a result of Americans' unquestioned allegiance to and belief in the purity and integrity of American institutions.

— Robin F. Bachin, Ph.D., University of Miami

unscathed: *unharmed*

After all these years, should Joe Jackson's incredible batting average allow him access to the Hall of Fame? Why?

10   9   8   7   6

PLAYING Fair?

The following descriptive list shows that unfortunately, fixed sports events did not end with the White Sox scandal.

1

In 2006, one of the largest soccer fixing scandals in Italian Series A, the top level of play, was uncovered by Italian police. Teams were accused of match fixing by selecting favorable referees. Four clubs were banned from participating in the 2006/2007 championships. Several others were demoted to the Series B league.

2

In 2005, a Brazilian sports magazine reported that two soccer referees were guilty of match fixing. Later, they confessed to taking bribes. Both referees were banned from the game.

3

Flockton Grey was an unremarkable two-year-old gelding that was set to run a race in 1982. His rider and owner ran a three-year-old horse in his place. The older and more experienced horse won by 20 lengths, which aroused the suspicion of the bookmakers. They refused to pay out the bets. A police investigation later revealed the truth. This was one of the largest betting scandals in British horse-racing history.

4

Jacob L. Molinas, an American pro basketball player, was a major figure in a scandal that almost destroyed NCAA basketball in the early 1950s. He and other players took bribes from mobsters in return for guaranteeing that their team wouldn't do well.

Take Note

Like Tourist Guy, this hoax was witnessed by a great number of people and there was nothing amusing about it. Because of the huge impact this World Series had on the lives and careers of a number of baseball players and the image of the game, this hoax comes in at #4.

- Compare the behavior of the baseball players with another hoaxer described so far. How are they different? Similar?

5   4   3   2   1

Robert Pilatus (left) and Fabrice Morvan of Milli Vanilli pose with their Best New Artist Grammys in 1990.

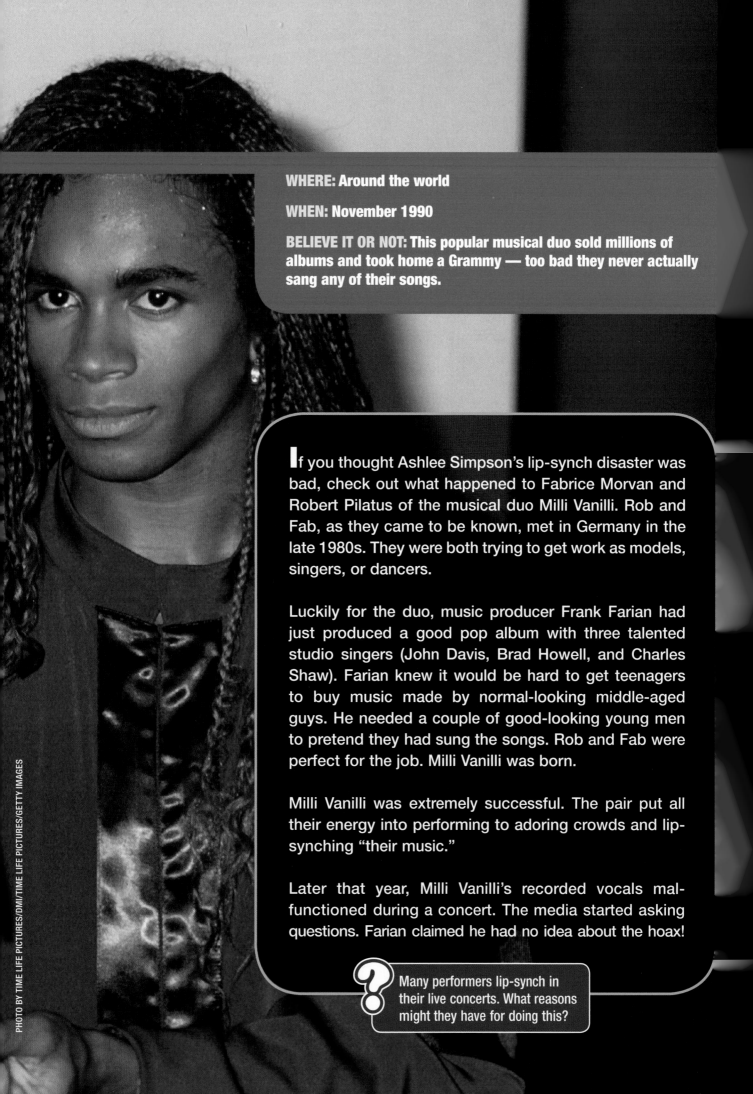

WHERE: Around the world

WHEN: November 1990

BELIEVE IT OR NOT: This popular musical duo sold millions of albums and took home a Grammy — too bad they never actually sang any of their songs.

If you thought Ashlee Simpson's lip-synch disaster was bad, check out what happened to Fabrice Morvan and Robert Pilatus of the musical duo Milli Vanilli. Rob and Fab, as they came to be known, met in Germany in the late 1980s. They were both trying to get work as models, singers, or dancers.

Luckily for the duo, music producer Frank Farian had just produced a good pop album with three talented studio singers (John Davis, Brad Howell, and Charles Shaw). Farian knew it would be hard to get teenagers to buy music made by normal-looking middle-aged guys. He needed a couple of good-looking young men to pretend they had sung the songs. Rob and Fab were perfect for the job. Milli Vanilli was born.

Milli Vanilli was extremely successful. The pair put all their energy into performing to adoring crowds and lip-synching "their music."

Later that year, Milli Vanilli's recorded vocals malfunctioned during a concert. The media started asking questions. Farian claimed he had no idea about the hoax!

? Many performers lip-synch in their live concerts. What reasons might they have for doing this?

MILLI VANILLI

Several lawsuits were filed claiming the group's record label defrauded consumers.

WHY IT HAPPENED

It was set up to sell records, of course! Frank Farian needed two attractive, energetic young artists for the album he had already made. And Rob and Fab were looking for a job, seeking fame and publicity. What a coincidence!

Knowing they would be found out sooner or later, Rob and Fab asked Farian to let them record their next album. Farian refused, and when the hoax was revealed, he told the media that Rob and Fab had planned the whole thing without his knowledge.

Quick Fact

How dare they? At one point Rob told *TIME* magazine that he and Fab sang as well as Elvis Presley, Bob Dylan, Paul McCartney, and Mick Jagger.

THE CLUES

Rob and Fab spoke with thick accents, but sang in flawless English. At a live concert, the record started skipping, revealing that they were lip-synching. Well before this incident, one of the three original album singers revealed Milli Vanilli's secret to the press, but later took back his statement.

BUSTED!

Rob and Fab were publicly ridiculed everywhere. Tragically, Rob eventually turned to drugs and died from an overdose.

Quick Fact

The Milli Vanilli song "Girl, You Know It's True" went six times platinum in the United States. After the hoax was exposed, the album was deleted from the recording company's catalog. It was the biggest-selling album ever taken out of print.

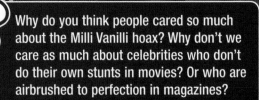

? Why do you think people cared so much about the Milli Vanilli hoax? Why don't we care as much about celebrities who don't do their own stunts in movies? Or who are airbrushed to perfection in magazines?

The Expert Says...

"Milli Vanilli became martyrs to this myth of authenticity. They were the recording industry's sacrifice meant to prove the integrity of their product. ...

— Ted Friedman, associate professor of communications at Georgia State University

10   9   8   7   6

The Rise and Fall of Milli Vanilli

This timeline follows Milli Vanilli through the good and the bad.

1980s	Rob and Fab, hired by Farian, become Milli Vanilli.
1988	"All Or Nothing" is released in Europe and is an instant success.
1989	*All or Nothing* is retitled *Girl You Know It's True* and released in the U.S.; it sells seven million copies.
1990	Milli Vanilli wins a Grammy for Best New Artist, in February.
1990	In November, Frank Farian reveals Milli Vanilli is a hoax and their Grammy is taken away.
1993	Comeback album as Rob and Fab fails; only 2,000 copies are sold.
1995	Rob is arrested in Los Angeles for assault and vandalism. He serves several months in jail.
2000	Fab is featured in a BBC documentary on Milli Vanilli.
2003	Fab releases his first solo album, *Love Revolution*. The critics approve.
2006	Fab releases a second solo album called *Roll*.

Take Note

Like two of the previous hoaxes — Alien Autopsy and Swiss Spaghetti Harvest — this hoax involved the use of media broadcasting to deceive an unsuspecting public. The hoax was so good that audiences everywhere were tricked and the pair was even celebrated with the music industry's highest award: a Grammy.

• Go online and do some research about other lip-synching incidents. Should these artists have been as shamed in the media as Milli Vanilli? Why?

5   4   **3**   2   1

He's not pretending this time! In this photo, master impostor Ferdinand Demara sits in jail.

LDO DEMARA

PHOTO BY HANK WALKER/TIME LIFE PICTURES/GETTY IMAGES

WHERE: Canada, the United States, and elsewhere

WHEN: 1950s

BELIEVE IT OR NOT: Demara (aka "The Great Impostor") successfully fooled almost everyone, almost all of the time.

Demara was the ultimate impostor! He lived the lives of a string of other people and faked their identities. He pretended to be a civil engineer, a sheriff's deputy, an assistant prison warden, a lawyer, a preacher, a teacher, a child-care expert, and even a naval surgeon.

He was born Ferdinand Waldo Demara in Massachusetts in 1921. Demara never graduated from high school. He left school to become a monk. When he did not like the secluded life of the monastery, he decided to join the U.S. Army. He didn't stay long in the military, though. When he didn't get the promotions he wanted, he moved again, and again.

Demara was a clever man with a very good memory. He was able to quickly learn the information he needed to make his various faked personalities come to life. He was so good that nobody suspected a thing. His employers were satisfied with his work, and he gained the respect of his colleagues.

Then came Demara's most famous identity theft — as Dr. Joseph Cyr, a surgeon in the Royal Canadian Navy. His success as a military doctor turned out to be his downfall. The mother of the real Dr. Cyr read about him in the newspapers …

FERDINAND WALDO DEMARA

WHY IT HAPPENED

No one knows for sure. Maybe he enjoyed acting. Or he was easily bored and needed lots of new challenges. When asked "why?" Demara answered, "Rascality, pure rascality." Surprisingly, even though Demara was dishonest, he never caused anyone harm with his lies.

THE CLUES

There really weren't many clues. After word got out about his many impersonations, it became harder and harder for Demara to get away with them.

---

rascality: *behaving like a rascal or troublemaker*

Quick Fact
Tony Curtis starred in the movie *The Great Impostor*, which was based on Demara's life.

Quick Fact
Demara died of heart failure on June 8, 1982. According to his obituary in *The New York Times*, he had spent part of the last eight years of his life working as a Baptist minister, and then as a visiting counselor at a hospital.

BUSTED!

News of the impostor became known when the identity of Dr. Cyr was revealed. Demara made things worse when he sold his story to a magazine. It became more and more difficult for him to continue his life as an impostor. It was reported that he had been arrested for theft, embezzlement, and forgery during his life. He even spent six months in prison for impersonating a teacher.

---

embezzlement: *wrongful use of money in one's care*

In what ways was Demara both a success and a failure?

The Expert Says...

"In a sense, all the impostors we read about are failures — a truly successful impostor will never become known as such."

— Robert Fulford, journalist

DEMARA'S UNMASKING

Want more dirt on how Demara was busted? Read the following report.

Demara actually saved lives when he impersonated a Canadian naval surgeon!

Demara posed as a monk when he visited Dr. Cyr, an experienced Canadian surgeon. He studied details of the doctor's life and stole his medical credentials. So when this seemingly very well qualified doctor volunteered for service in the Canadian navy in March 1951, they snapped him up. They did not even check his references or qualifications. Skilled surgeons were desperately needed in the navy.

Hopefully, Demara's monk disguise was better than this!

Demara was assigned to the HMCS *Cayuga* and went on duty in Korea. He successfully amputated a leg and removed bullets from injured men. How did he do it? He studied medical texts the night before and then performed surgeries with no reported problems. In fact, he was being considered for an award for his outstanding work in the navy when he was found out.

? How would you feel if you had been a friend or colleague of Demara's and later found out he was an impostor?

The real Dr. Cyr's mother read a newspaper article about this exceptional surgeon and quickly revealed Demara to be an impostor. Her own son was living in New Brunswick at that time. The men on his ship could not believe it. The navy dismissed Demara because of his faked identity, but they never discovered he wasn't a doctor. This might help to explain why Demara was discharged from the navy without punishment. Demara went on to assume many more faked identities until his death.

Take Note

The impersonations of Milli Vanilli and Ferdinand Waldo Demara were widely reported by the media. They all deceived the public and made money from their daring deceptions. However, Demara's impersonations needed greater skill and intelligence because he had to keep reinventing himself every day of his life.

- Do some research online to come up with three other stories of famous impostors. Why do you think society condemns these people?

DEMARA PHOTO-© BETTMANN/CORBIS; ALL OTHER IMAGES-ISTOCKPHOTO, SHUTTERSTOCK.

5 4 3 **2** 1

THE WAR OF

Artist's interpretation of
The War of the Worlds

THE WORLDS

WHERE: A radio studio in New York

WHEN: October 30, 1938

BELIEVE IT OR NOT: A radio broadcast convinced as many as six million listeners that Martians had invaded the world.

It is probably the most famous broadcast in radio history. The regularly scheduled music show was interrupted many times with announcements about a Martian invasion of Earth.

"… A huge, flaming object, believed to be a meteorite, fell on a farm. … Ladies and gentlemen, this is the most terrifying thing I have ever witnessed. … The eyes are black and gleam like a serpent … a jet of flame springing from that mirror, and it leaps right at the advancing men. It strikes them head on! Good Lord, they're turning into flame!"

Listeners heard what appeared to them to be a live broadcast of news of a Martian invasion in New Jersey. They were horrified.

It was reported in the newspapers the next day that some people experienced heart attacks; others jammed into the New York City bus terminal as they tried to flee to safety. In their panic, these people were trying to escape the Martians and their poisonous gas!

Today, we know that these newspaper accounts were greatly exaggerated, and the whole episode was a hoax.

 If you turned on the radio and heard this dramatic reporting, would you believe it was real? Why or why not?

THE WAR OF THE WORLDS

WHY IT HAPPENED

On October 30, 1938, Orson Welles's Mercury Theatre on the Air dramatized H. G. Wells's book *The War of the Worlds* on its one-hour radio show. Nobody knew the real reason. Perhaps it was a project to look into the effects of mass media on radio listeners. Or, maybe the famous Mercury Theatre radio program just wanted to entertain their listeners with a dramatic reading of H.G. Wells's famous novel. Whatever the reason, the radio station and the police were unprepared for the number of distressed callers.

? What lessons about human nature does the impact of this hoax reveal?

Quick Fact

It was reported that, at first, some listeners thought the radio announcement of the bombing of Pearl Harbor in 1945 was a fake similar to the *War of the Worlds* broadcast in 1938.

Quick Fact

Apparently, 25 percent of the listeners believed what they heard on the broadcast. But most young people were not fooled because they recognized Orson Welles's voice as that of The Shadow, a favorite radio hero.

THE CLUES

The broadcast was introduced as fiction, and there were reminders of this during the show (even if they were few and far between). Another clue is that no other radio station was interrupting programming to alert listeners to the invasion.

BUSTED!

There was a public outcry, but the radio studio and The Mercury Theatre escaped punishment because they had made announcements about the piece being a work of fiction. However, the radio studio had to promise to never again use the "we interrupt this program" intro for anything other than real news.

The Expert Says...

> With the world on the threshold of war, anxiety regarding such [news] bulletins was laced with a fear that the next one might indicate the start of hostilities.

— Dr. Paul Heyer, professor, Wilfrid Laurier University

10   9   8   7   6

REAL-LIFE ALIEN INVASION?

Orson Welles's broadcast of a Martian landing was so convincing that it caused a nationwide panic! People really believed that the Martians had landed! Here is an excerpt from the original script:

ANNOUNCER:

Now I look down the harbor. All manner of boats, overloaded with fleeing population, pulling out from docks.

Streets are all jammed. Noise in crowds like New Year's Eve in city. Wait a minute ... The ... the enemy is now in sight above the Palisades. Five — five great machines. First one is crossing the river. I can see it from here, wading ... wading the Hudson like a man wading through a brook ...

A bulletin is handed me ... Martian cylinders are falling all over the country. One outside of Buffalo, one in Chicago ... St. Louis ... seem to be timed and spaced ...

Now the first machine reaches the shore. He stands watching, looking over the city. His steel, cowlish head is even with the skyscrapers. He waits for the others. They rise like a line of new towers on the city's west side ...

Now they're lifting their metal hands. This is the end now. Smoke comes out ... black smoke, drifting over the city. People in the streets see it now. They're running towards the East River ... thousands of them, dropping in like rats.

Now the smoke's spreading faster. It's reached Times Square. People are trying to run away from it, but it's no use. They're falling like flies.

Now the smoke's crossing Sixth Avenue ... Fifth Avenue ... a ... a hundred yards away ... it's fifty feet ...

(BODY FALLS)
(SOUNDS OF CITY IN TURMOIL, FOGHORNS, WHISTLES ...)

cowlish: *hood-like*

Orson Welles and the Mercury Theatre Orchestra

Take Note

Welles's broadcast of *The War of the Worlds* required careful planning, great cleverness, and enormous daring. The hoax had an immediate and huge impact on the millions of listeners that tuned in to the program that day. That's why this hoax ranks #1 on our list.

• Welles's broadcast simulated reality. Some people say that our lives today are overwhelmed with imitations. Referring to the other hoaxes in this book, as well as to your own experience, would you agree?

5   4   3   2   **1**

We Thought …

Here are some of the criteria we used in ranking the 10 most outrageous hoaxes.

The hoax:

- Spread to a large number of people via the World Wide Web or mass media
- Became a pop-culture sensation
- Fooled a lot of people
- Developed into a scandal
- Took advantage of people
- Was developed for personal and financial gain
- Required considerable skills and cleverness
- Was original and creative
- Had an impact on a large number of people

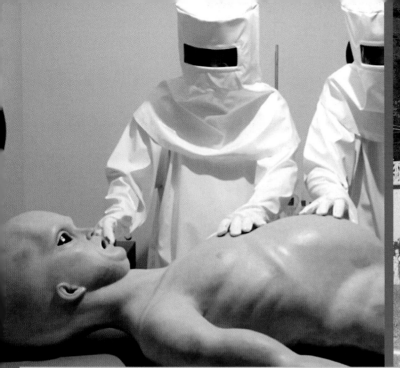

What Do You Think?

1. Do you agree with our ranking? If you don't, try ranking them yourself. Justify your ranking with data from your own research and reasoning. You may refer to our criteria, or you may want to draw up your own list of criteria.

2. Here are three other hoaxes that we considered but in the end did not include in our top 10 list: the Piltdown man, the Howard Hughes biography, and the Hitler diaries.
   - Find out more about them. Do you think they should have made our list? Give reasons for your response.
   - Are there other outrageous hoaxes that you think should have made our list? Explain your choices.

Index